step-by-step cooking

KOREAN

delightful ideas for everyday meals

Lee MinJung

Marshall Cavendish
Cuisine

The Publisher wishes to thank Sia Huat Pte Ltd for the loan of their crockery and utensils.

Photographer: Sam Yeo
Food Preparation: Gourmet Haven

First published 2005 as Feast of Flavours from the Korean Kitchen
This new edition 2009

Published by Marshall Cavendish Cuisine
An imprint of Marshall Cavendish International
1 New Industrial Road, Singapore 536196

Other Marshall Cavendish Offices:
Marshall Cavendish Ltd. 5th Floor, 32-38 Saffron Hill, London EC1N 8FH, UK ▪ Marshall
Cavendish Corporation. 99 White Plains Road, Tarrytown NY 10591-9001, USA ▪ Marshall
Cavendish International (Thailand) Co Ltd. 253 Asoke, 12th Flr, Sukhumvit 21 Road, Klongtoey
Nua, Wattana, Bangkok 10110, Thailand ▪ Marshall Cavendish (Malaysia) Sdn Bhd, Times
Subang, Lot 46, Subang Hi-Tech Industrial Park, Batu Tiga, 40000 Shah Alam, Selangor Darul
Ehsan, Malaysia.

Marshall Cavendish is a trademark of Times Publishing Limited

National Library Board Singapore Cataloguing in Publication Data

Lee, MinJung, 1970-
Korean : delightful ideas for everyday meals / Lee MinJung. – New ed. – Singapore :
Marshall Cavendish Cuisine, 2009.
p. cm. – (Step-by-step cooking series)
ISBN-13 : 978-981-261-799-6
ISBN-10 : 981-261-799-X

1. Cookery, Korean. I. Title. II. Series: Step-by-step cooking series (Marshall Cavendish Cuisine)

TX724.5.K65
641.59519 -- dc22   OCN320053134

Printed in Singapore by Times Printers Pte Ltd

CONTENTS

COOKING TECHNIQUES

MARINATING

This is a popular technique used all over the world to flavour and tenderise meat prior to cooking it. In Korea, pineapple syrup and pear juice are commonly used to tenderise beef and pork while marinating. Pineapple syrup can be obtained from canned pineapples. Pear juice is available from Korean supermarkets, but you can also grate a pear and extract the juice. Spring onions are also a common marinating agent in Korean cooking, to lend flavour to the cooked dish.

STIR-FRYING

Stir-frying is a quick and fuss-free method of cooking. If you do not have a wok, a large frying pan will suffice. Ensure that the pan is hot before adding in the cooking oil. Allow the cooking oil to heat up before adding in your ingredients. Stir them around quickly with a spatula to heat them through. Once the food is cooked, dish out and serve hot.

Because the stir-frying process is so quick, you need to have all the ingredients prepared and on hand before heating up the wok. This will ensure that the ingredients do not overcook or burn as you are busy with other ingredients.

Note: When stir-frying seafood, toss it quickly to cook. This will seal in the juices without overcooking the seafood. Overcooked seafood will be tough.

INTRODUCTION

BRAISING

This cooking technique is similar to stewing, where meat is cooked slowly in liquid, in order to tenderise and add flavour to the meat. In braising, it is important that the vegetables and meat are cut to a similar size so they cook more evenly. In some recipes, the meat is first seared to seal in the juices and to add colour, before water is added to the pot for braising over low heat.

GRILLING (BROILING)

Grilling is done by setting food above or below a heat source to cook it. This can be done over hot coals/charcoal, under the electric grill, in the oven or even on the top of the stove using a heavy-based pan. For successful grilling, the heat must be well-regulated so the food doesn't burn or blacken on the outside too readily while remaining raw on the inside. Grilling lends a unique barbecued flavour to cooked dishes.

STEAMING

In steaming, the ingredients are cooked by the vapour that rises from the boiling liquid below. As the ingredients do not come in direct contact with the liquid, most of the nutrients are retained, making this a healthy means of cooking food. To get the best results out of steaming food, always use the freshest ingredients.

To steam food, place the ingredients in a heatproof plate or container and place over boiling liquid. Cover tightly with a lid to keep the steam in.

PICKLING

In Korea, pickling was done out of necessity to preserve food for the cold winter months. Today, kimchi continues to be enjoyed both as a side dish and an appetiser in Korea, and it is served at almost every meal. In pickling, the vegetable, (most commonly cabbage, white radish or cucumber), is first salted to prevent spoilage then seasoned with ingredients such as chilli, garlic, ginger, soy sauce and spring onions. As the vegetable matures, it becomes tender but retains its crunchiness.

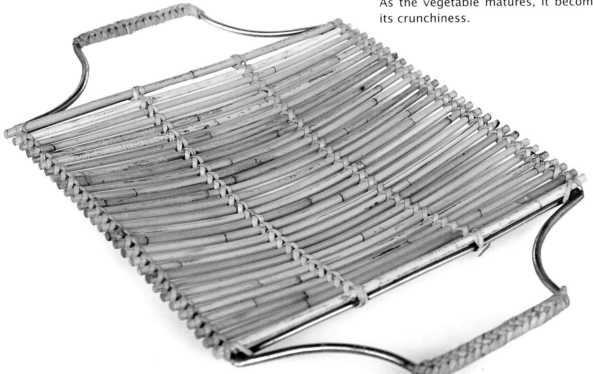

COOKING UTENSILS

Korean cooking is relatively simple and no special equipment is necessary. For stir-frying, any type of wok or pan used in other cuisines can be used, together with any type of spatula. Even in the preparation of kimchi, Korean homes will today use any type of vessel even though earthenware jars were used traditionally.

This is a list of equipment used either in the Korean kitchen or at the Korean table today. Some of these utensils are common to many other cuisines and cultures as well.

SERVING TRAY

Wooden trays were traditionally used for serving meals consisting of several dishes, such as rice or noodles, side dishes and soups. These wooden trays have foldable legs so the dishes stand higher on the table, at a more comfortable height for the diner.

CHOPSTICKS AND SPOONS

Traditional Korean chopsticks and spoons are made of copper, brass or silver. Today, they are commonly made of stainless steel and silver. Korean chopsticks are long and thin, and because they are made of metal, are generally heavier than Chinese or Japanese chopsticks. Korean spoons have long, thin handles and round heads. The chopsticks are used for picking out food from side dishes and the spoon is used for scooping up rice and soup.

**MULTI-SECTIONED TRAY
(GU-JEOL-PAN)**

This multi-sectioned tray is made of wood and decorated with delicate floral motifs. In an elaborate Korean meal, it is used to serve the first course of thin pancakes with various fillings.

SPATULA

There are various types of spatulas and they are useful for stirring, turning or lifting food from pans and woks. When using non-stick pans or woks, use non-stick spatulas or wooden spatulas to avoid damaging the pan or wok. Slotted spatulas like this one pictured here are useful for draining liquids or fats from food when removing food from the pan or wok. When choosing a spatula, find one that fits into the palm of your hand comfortably to allow for ease of use.

HOT POT (TTUK-BAE-GI)

This is a glazed clay pot with a cover, used for cooking soups and stews. Like the clay pot that the Chinese use, it can be placed directly over a flame. Hot pots can be taken off the fire and brought directly to the table to continue keeping the food in it warm throughout the meal.

SIEVE

In baking, sieves are used for aerating flours or removing lumps from flour. In cooking, sieves are useful for separating solids from liquids. Sieves are made from a variety of materials—wooden frames and nylon or metal mesh, plastic frames with nylon mesh and fully stainless steel sieves. It is useful to have a few sieves on hand so you will always have a clean, dry sieve available when another is in use or has just been washed.

COLANDER

Colanders are large bowls with many holes that, like sieves, are useful for separating solids from liquids. Larger colanders will have legs or a base to stand on, so water can drain right through and the solids at the base are not left soaking in the liquid. This colander pictured here is collapsible, and is ideal for storage when space is tight.

WEIGHTS & MEASURES

Quantities for this book are given in Metric, Imperial and American (spoon and cup) measures. Standard spoon and cup measurements used are: 1 tsp = 5 ml, 1 Tbsp = 15 ml, 1 cup = 250 ml. All measures are level unless otherwise stated.

Liquid And Volume Measures

Metric	Imperial	American
5 ml	1/6 fl oz	1 teaspoon
10 ml	1/3 fl oz	1 dessertspoon
15 ml	1/2 fl oz	1 tablespoon
60 ml	2 fl oz	1/4 cup (4 tablespoons)
85 ml	2 1/2 fl oz	1/3 cup
90 ml	3 fl oz	3/8 cup (6 tablespoons)
125 ml	4 fl oz	1/2 cup
180 ml	6 fl oz	3/4 cup
250 ml	8 fl oz	1 cup
300 ml	10 fl oz (1/2 pint)	1 1/4 cups
375 ml	12 fl oz	1 1/2 cups
435 ml	14 fl oz	1 3/4 cups
500 ml	16 fl oz	2 cups
625 ml	20 fl oz (1 pint)	2 1/2 cups
750 ml	24 fl oz (1 1/5 pints)	3 cups
1 litre	32 fl oz (1 3/5 pints)	4 cups
1.25 litres	40 fl oz (2 pints)	5 cups
1.5 litres	48 fl oz (2 2/5 pints)	6 cups
2.5 litres	80 fl oz (4 pints)	10 cups

Dry Measures

Metric	Imperial
30 grams	1 ounce
45 grams	1 1/2 ounces
55 grams	2 ounces
70 grams	2 1/2 ounces
85 grams	3 ounces
100 grams	3 1/2 ounces
110 grams	4 ounces
125 grams	4 1/2 ounces
140 grams	5 ounces
280 grams	10 ounces
450 grams	16 ounces (1 pound)
500 grams	1 pound, 1 1/2 ounces
700 grams	1 1/2 pounds
800 grams	1 3/4 pounds
1 kilogram	2 pounds, 3 ounces
1.5 kilograms	3 pounds, 4 1/2 ounces
2 kilograms	4 pounds, 6 ounces

Oven Temperature

	°C	°F	Gas Regulo
Very slow	120	250	1
Slow	150	300	2
Moderately slow	160	325	3
Moderate	180	350	4
Moderately hot	190/200	375/400	5/6
Hot	210/220	410/425	6/7
Very hot	230	450	8
Super hot	250/290	475/550	9/10

Length

Metric	Imperial
0.5 cm	1/4 inch
1 cm	1/2 inch
1.5 cm	3/4 inch
2.5 cm	1 inch

Abbreviation

tsp	teaspoon
Tbsp	tablespoon
g	gram
kg	kilogram
ml	millilitre

SOUPS & STEWS

Seaweed Soup *(Mi-Yeok-Guk)*

Soy Bean Paste Stew *(Doen-Jang-Jji-Kae)*

Kimchi Stew *(Kim-Chi-Jji-Kae)*

Spicy Soft Bean Curd Stew *(Sun-Du-Bu-Jji-Kae)*

Spicy Fish Stew *(Mae-Woon-Tang)*

Chicken Ginseng Stew *(Sam-Gye-Tang)*

Mushroom Stew with Vegetables *(Beo-Seot-Jeon-Gol)*

SEAWEED SOUP (MI-YEOK-GUK)

Seaweed in a beef or clam stock. This soup is traditionally served during birthday celebrations and to women after childbirth.

INGREDIENTS

Dried seaweed	55 g (2 oz), soaked in cold water for 10 minutes
Sesame oil	1/2 Tbsp
Crushed garlic	1 tsp
Beef or shelled clams	500 g (1 lb 1 1/2 oz), diced
Water	2.5–3 litres (80–96 fl oz / 10–12 cups)
Korean soy sauce or fish sauce	to taste

METHOD

- Drain seaweed and cut into smaller pieces.

- Heat sesame oil in a pan and add crushed garlic, seaweed, beef or clams. Stir-fry over high heat for 5 minutes.

- Add water and bring to the boil. Reduce heat to low and simmer for 40–50 minutes.

- Add soy sauce or fish sauce to taste. Serve in individual bowls.

Squeeze any excess water from seaweed before placing on a cutting board to cut.

Stir-frying the garlic, seaweed and meat will help mix the ingredients while making them more fragrant.

Pour just enough water to fill the pan. The amount will depend on the size of the pan used. Add more water as it evaporates.

SOY BEAN PASTE STEW (DOEN-JANG-JJI-KAE)

This lightly spicy stew is flavoured with dried anchovies and fermented soy bean paste.

INGREDIENTS

Water	435 ml (14 fl oz / 1³/₄ cups)
Dried anchovies	100 g (3¹/₂ oz)
Fermented soy paste (*doen-jang*)	3 Tbsp
Firm bean curd	180 g (6¹/₂ oz), cut into 1-cm (¹/₂-in) cubes
Green chilli	1, sliced and seeded
Crushed garlic	¹/₂ Tbsp
Courgette (zucchini)	1, small, sliced
Potatoes	150 g (5¹/₃ oz), peeled and sliced
Chilli powder	1 tsp
Spring onions (scallions)	2, sliced

METHOD

- Bring water to the boil and add dried anchovies. Leave to boil for 20 minutes to make a stock.

- Strain stock into an earthen bowl or clay pot. Discard anchovies.

- Add fermented soy paste and stir to dissolve.

- Reduce heat to medium, then add all remaining ingredients except chilli powder and spring onions. Cook for about 10 minutes, then stir in chilli powder.

- Garnish with spring onions and serve hot.

Slice the chillies lengthwise to remove the seeds so the stew will not be too spicy. Cut the chillies into smaller pieces.

You can either use a sieve to strain the stock or use a spoon to hold back the anchovies while pouring the stock into the clay pot.

Gently lower the ingredients into the boiling stock to avoid being scalded by the stock.

KIMCHI STEW (KIM-CHI-JJI-KAE)

This spicy and sour kimchi stew is made more substantial with the addition of pork.

INGREDIENTS

Pork	100 g (3^1/$_2$ oz), thinly sliced
Ginger juice	1 tsp
Light soy sauce	2 tsp
Ground black pepper	1 tsp
Sugar	1 tsp
Kimchi brine (see Note)	250 ml (8 fl oz / 1 cup)
Sour kimchi	200 g (7 oz), cut into 2-cm (1-in) cubes
Water	375 ml (12 fl oz / 1^1/$_2$ cups)
Soft bean curd	1 block, sliced
Leek slices	

METHOD

- Season pork with ginger juice, soy sauce, black pepper, sugar and kimchi brine for 20 minutes.

- Place seasoned pork with sour kimchi in a pot. Pour in water and bring to the boil.

- Reduce heat and add bean curd. Simmer for 20 minutes.

- Garnish with leek slices and serve hot.

Note: Kimchi comes soaked in brine. Drain the brine for use in recipes such as this one.

Use a sharp knife to slice the pork into thin slices.

Use a small bowl when seasoning small amounts of pork.

Place bean curd slices gently into the pot so they do not break up and look unappetising.

SPICY SOFT BEAN CURD STEW
(SUN-DU-BU-JJI-KAE)

A hot and spicy bean curd stew with kimchi and egg.

INGREDIENTS

Red chilli oil	1 Tbsp
Crushed garlic	1 Tbsp
Chilli powder	1 Tbsp
Light soy sauce	1 tsp
Beef seasoning powder	$1/2$ Tbsp
Onion	50 g (1$^2/_3$ oz), peeled and diced
Kimchi	30 g (1 oz), chopped
Pork	50 g (1$^2/_3$ oz), sliced
Water	250 ml (8 fl oz / 1 cup)
Silken or egg bean curd	1 tube (140 g / 5 oz), sliced into rounds
Egg	1
Spring onion (scallion)	1, sliced or a few slices of leek

METHOD

- Heat an empty earthen bowl or clay pot until it becomes very hot. Reduce heat and add in chilli oil, crushed garlic, chilli powder, soy sauce, beef seasoning powder, onion, kimchi and pork. Stir-fry for 5 minutes.

- Pour in water and bring to the boil. Carefully slide in bean curd rounds without breaking them. Simmer over low heat for 10–15 minutes.

- Crack egg into stew and remove from heat. Sprinkle spring onion or leek slices over and serve.

Roasting ingredients in an earthen bowl or clay pot will help bring out their flavour.

Use a palette knife to gently slide the bean curd rounds into the stew so as not to break them.

Crack the egg directly into the stew. Alternatively, crack it into a bowl, then pour it in. The residual heat from the stew will cook the egg.

SPICY FISH STEW (MAE-WOON-TANG)

This spicy fish and vegetable stew makes a hearty meal with white rice.

Combine stock ingredients in a pot, then add in water and bring to the boil.

Cut the fish through into 3 or 4 pieces. Use a sharp knife and hold the fish down firmly when doing this.

Chrysanthemum leaves wilt easily when in contact with heat. Add them to the hot dish just before serving.

INGREDIENTS

Ginger juice	2 tsp
Salt	1 tsp
Ground white pepper	1 tsp
Red snapper or cod	1, medium-size, cut into large pieces
Courgette (zucchini)	30 g (1 oz), cut into 2-cm (1-in) squares
Carrot	30 g (1 oz), cut into 2-cm (1-in) squares
Red chilli	1, sliced
Chrysanthemum leaves	2 small stalks, cut into 3-cm (1$\frac{1}{2}$-in) lengths (optional)

STOCK

Dried anchovies	30 g (1 oz)
Dried kelp	10 x 10-cm (5 x 5-in) piece
White radish	100 g (3$\frac{1}{2}$ oz)
Onion	100 g (3$\frac{1}{2}$ oz)
Water	2.5 litres (80 fl oz / 10 cups)

SEASONING

Red chilli paste	2 Tbsp
Chilli powder	1 Tbsp
Crushed garlic	1 Tbsp
Salt	1 tsp
Ground white pepper	1 tsp
Sugar	1 tsp

METHOD

- Prepare stock. Combine ingredients for stock in a pot and cook over medium heat for 40 minutes. When stock is cooking, marinate fish.

- Sprinkle ginger juice, salt and pepper over fish. Leave for 30 minutes.

- Combine seasoning ingredients and mix well.

- When stock is ready, strain and discard solids. Return stock to the boil and add courgette, carrot, chilli, fish and seasoning. Cook for 10 minutes.

- Serve hot with chrysanthemum leaves, if using.

CHICKEN GINSENG STEW (SAM-GYE-TANG)

Chicken stuffed with ginseng, glutinous rice and garlic then stewed to perfection.

INGREDIENTS

Whole chicken	1, about 1–1.5 kg (2 lb 3 oz–3 lb 4¹/₂ oz)
Korean ginseng	8-cm (3-in) piece
Glutinous rice	90 g (3 oz), soaked for 1 hour
Garlic	6 cloves, peeled
Water	3 litres (96 fl oz / 12 cups)
Dried red dates	2
Chestnuts	2, peeled
Salt	to taste
Ground white pepper	to taste

METHOD

- Clean chicken and discard organs. Cut off and discard head, feet, wing tips and neck. Leave body whole. Clean and wash thoroughly.

- Skewer neck with toothpicks or bamboo skewers, then stuff chicken with ginseng, rice and garlic.

- Sew rear end of chicken up to hold stuffing in.

- Put stuffed chicken into a pot. Add water, cover and bring to the boil.

- Lower heat and add red dates and chestnuts. Simmer until chicken is tender.

- Remove toothpicks or skewers and serve hot. Allow guests to add salt and pepper to taste.

Hold the chicken firmly down on a cutting board and cut the wing tips off with a sharp knife.

Seal the neck cavity using toothpicks or bamboo skewers.

Fill the chicken cavity with stuffing ingredients.

MUSHROOM STEW WITH VEGETABLES
(BEO-SEOT-JEON-GOL)

A rich casserole of beef, mushrooms, leek and carrot.

INGREDIENTS

Beef	225 g (8 oz), cut into thin strips
Onion	1, peeled and sliced
Leek	1, sliced
Carrot	1/2, sliced
Red chillies	2, sliced
Shiitake mushrooms	5, stems discarded and sliced
Enokitake mushrooms	100 g (3 1/2 oz), base trimmed
Oyster mushrooms	100 g (3 1/2 oz), torn into shreds
Hon shimeji mushrooms	70 g (2 1/2 oz), base trimmed and sliced
Water or beef stock	750 ml (24 fl oz / 3 cups)
Salt or light soy sauce	to taste

MARINADE

Light soy sauce	1 Tbsp
Minced garlic	2 tsp
Ground black pepper	2 tsp
Sugar	1 tsp
Sesame oil	1 Tbsp

METHOD

- Combine ingredients for marinade in a bowl. Add beef and mix well.

- Arrange beef, onion, leek, carrot, chillies and mushrooms neatly in a 5-cm (2-in) deep, heavy-based pan or casserole dish.

- Pour in water or beef stock, then sprinkle with salt or light soy sauce. Bring to the boil before serving. Garnish as desired.

Note: At the table, mix the ingredients up before ladling into individual serving bowls. Eat with rice.

Shred the oyster mushrooms with your hands.

Arrange the prepared ingredients in the pan or casserole dish attractively.

Pour the water or stock gently over the ingredients so as not to spoil the arrangement.

29

VEGETABLES & SALADS

Bean Sprout Salad (Kong-Na-Mul-Mu-Chim)

Radish Salad (Mu-Saeng-Chae)

Seasoned Spinach (Si-Geum-Chi-Mu-Chim)

Braised Pan-fried Bean Curd (Du-Bu-Jo-Rim)

Whole Cabbage Kimchi (Kim-Chi)

Watery Radish Kimchi (Na-Bak-Kim-Chi)

Stuffed Cucumber Kimchi (O-E-So-Bae-Gi)

Diced Radish Kimchi (Kkak-Du-Gi)

Pan-fried Stuffed Chillies (Go-Chu-Jeon)

BEAN SPROUT SALAD
(KONG-NA-MUL-MU-CHIM)

This is a refreshing dish of crisp and nutritious soy bean sprouts.

INGREDIENTS

Water	3 Tbsp
Soy bean sprouts	300 g (11 oz), tailed and cleaned
Salt	as needed
Crushed garlic	1 tsp
White sesame seeds	$\frac{1}{2}$ Tbsp, roasted and finely ground
Spring onion (scallion)	1, chopped
Sesame oil	to taste

METHOD

- Place water and bean sprouts in a pan and sprinkle 1 tsp salt over. Place over medium heat, cover and leave bean sprouts to steam for 5–7 minutes.

- Mix steamed bean sprouts with crushed garlic, ground sesame seeds and spring onion. Adjust to taste with more salt and sesame oil. Serve cold.

Gently bend and break the tails off the bean sprouts.

Sprinkle the salt evenly over the bean sprouts using the tips of your fingers.

Mix the seasoning into the bean sprouts without bruising the bean sprouts by using a pair of chopsticks.

RADISH SALAD (MU-SAENG-CHAE)

This radish salad is both sweet and sour, with the use of sugar and vinegar.

INGREDIENTS

White radish	200 g (7 oz), peeled, then shredded or julienned
Salt	1 tsp
Sugar	1 Tbsp
White sesame seeds	$^1/_2$ tsp, roasted
Vinegar	2 Tbsp
Crushed garlic	1 tsp
Ginger juice	1 tsp
Sliced spring onion (scallion)	1 Tbsp
Red chilli	1, sliced (optional)

METHOD

Mix radish with salt and sugar to preserve it. Refrigerate for 3–4 hours.

- Drain radish of any juices and mix with sesame seeds, vinegar, crushed garlic, ginger juice and spring onion.

- Taste and add more salt and sugar as preferred. Serve cold, garnished with red chilli slices if desired.

Use a handheld vegetable grater to shred or julienne the radish.

Drain the radish well so the final dish will not be soggy.

Mix the ingredients thoroughly using a pair of chopsticks.

SEASONED SPINACH (SI-GEUM-CHI-MU-CHIM)

This simple side dish is made with boiled spinach. You can use any type of spinach for this recipe.

INGREDIENTS

Spinach	150 g (5$^1/_3$ oz), roots discarded, stalks and leaves separated
Crushed garlic	$^1/_2$ tsp
Salt	$^1/_2$ tsp
Sesame oil	$^1/_2$ tsp
White sesame seeds	$^1/_2$ tsp, roasted

METHOD

- Bring a pot of water to the boil and sprinkle in some salt. Place spinach in, stalks first. When stalks are almost done, add leaves. Remove from heat as soon as water returns to the boil again.

- Rinse spinach in ice cold water and drain. Squeeze out any excess water with your hands.

- Cut spinach into shorter sections and mix with crushed garlic, salt and sesame oil. Toss well, then sprinkle sesame seeds over.

- Serve or store for up to a day in the refrigerator.

Boil the stalks first. When they are almost tender, put the leaves in to cook. This will ensure that the leaves are not overcooked.

Place the boiled spinach in a bowl of cold water to retain its colour and crunchiness. Squeeze out any excess water.

Place spinach on a chopping board and cut into shorter lengths.

BRAISED PAN-FRIED BEAN CURD (DU-BU-JO-RIM)

Pan-fried bean curd covered in a lightly spicy sauce.

INGREDIENTS

Bean curd	1 block, sliced
Plain (all-purpose) flour	100 g (3½ oz / 1 cup)
Corn flour (cornstarch)	100 g (3½ oz / 1 cup)
Cooking oil	125 ml (4 fl oz / ½ cup)

SAUCE

Light soy sauce	4 Tbsp
Sugar	½ Tbsp
Chilli powder	1 Tbsp
Crushed garlic	1 tsp
Chopped spring onion (scallion)	2 tsp
Mirin	1 Tbsp
White sesame seeds	1 tsp, roasted

METHOD

- Coat bean curd slices with combined plain flour and corn flour mixture.

- Heat oil in a frying pan and pan-fry bean curd slices on one side until golden brown, then flip them over to fry the other side. Arrange on a serving plate.

- Combine ingredients for sauce and blend well. Pour sauce over hot bean curd pieces before serving.

Slice the bean curd into thin rectangular slices.

Handle the bean curd slices gently or they will break. Coat them well with a mixture of plain flour and corn flour.

Pan-fry the bean curd slices until golden brown on one side before flipping them over to cook the other side.

WHOLE CABBAGE KIMCHI (KIM-CHI)

This classic Korean kimchi is made with Chinese cabbage. It is served as a side dish with almost every meal in Korea.

INGREDIENTS

Chinese cabbage	2 heads, cut lengthwise in half
Coarse salt	300 g (11 oz / 2 cups)
Korean preserved prawns (shrimps)	90 g (3 oz / ½ cup)
Chilli powder	70 g (2½ oz / 1 cup)
Onion	100 g (3½ oz), peeled and chopped
Salt	2 Tbsp
Sugar	2 Tbsp
Garlic	7 cloves, peeled and minced
Ginger	2.5-cm (1-in) knob, peeled and minced
White radish	1, medium, julienned
Spring onions (scallions)	5, chopped or 2 stalks leek, chopped

METHOD

- Wilt cabbage by sprinkling liberally with coarse salt and letting it sit for 4 hours. Rinse cabbage thoroughly and drain well.

- Put preserved prawns with chilli powder, onion, salt, sugar, garlic and ginger in a blender and process. Transfer mixture to a bowl.

- Add radish and spring onion or leeks to bowl and mix well.

- Pack mixture between leaves of wilted cabbage.

- Place cabbage into airtight plastic containers or kimchi jars. Store at room temperature for 1–2 days before refrigerating. Use as required.

Make a cut halfway down the length of the cabbage, starting from the base. You can then pull the cabbage apart using both hands.

Wear a pair of gloves to protect your hands when packing the blended mixture between the cabbage leaves.

Roll the cabbage leaves up from the base towards the frilly part of the leaves. This will ensure that the blended mixture is held tightly between the leaves.

WATERY RADISH KIMCHI
(NA-BAK-KIM-CHI)

A refreshing and fragrant kimchi with a tangy juice. Unlike other types of kimchi, this recipe does not use chilli paste, so it is colourless.

INGREDIENTS

Chinese cabbage	1 head, cut into bite-size pieces
White radish	150 g (5$\frac{1}{3}$ oz), cut into rounds, then quartered
Salt	4 Tbsp
Garlic	2 cloves, peeled and chopped
Spring onions (scallions)	2, cut into 2-cm (1-in) lengths
Ginger	2 slices, chopped
Water	3.25 litres (104 fl oz / 13 cups)
Clear sweetened carbonated water (eg. Seven-Up or Sprite)	125 ml (4 fl oz / $\frac{1}{2}$ cup)

METHOD

- Combine cabbage and radish and sprinkle with salt. Leave to stand for 15–20 minutes, tossing the mixture occasionally.

- Rinse cabbage and radish in cold water to remove salt. Drain and mix with garlic, spring onions and ginger.

- Pour in water and carbonated water. You can also add some salt to taste if preferred.

- Cover and leave in a cool place for 3–4 days before serving cold. Garnish as desired.

Chop the garlic by first cutting into slices then chopping. This makes it easier to handle.

Cut the cabbage into bite-size pieces by making a cut two-thirds down from the tip of the leaves to the base. Then make multiple cuts across for smaller pieces.

Soak the cabbage in a mixture of water and sweetened carbonated water to preserve it.

STUFFED CUCUMBER KIMCHI
(O-E-SO-BAE-GI)

This simple stuffed cucumber dish is easy to prepare, but it must be refrigerated for 5–6 hours before serving.

Do not peel the cucumbers but simply rub them with salt to smoothen the skin.

INGREDIENTS

Japanese cucumbers	3
Kosher or sea salt	60 g (2 oz)

STUFFING

Chinese chives	45 g (1 1/2 oz), finely chopped
Carrot	30 g (1 oz), chopped
Garlic	3 cloves, peeled and chopped
Ginger	2 slices, chopped
Fish sauce	3 Tbsp
Chilli powder	2–2 1/2 Tbsp

Cut a cross on one side of cucumbers. The cut should go about halfway down the length of the cucumbers.

METHOD

- Smoothen cucumbers by rubbing with some salt.

- Cut 1 cm (1/2 in) off each end of cucumbers and discard. Slice cucumbers into 6–8-cm (2–3-in) lengths.

- Stand cucumbers on a cut side. Make a cut across one side of cucumbers but do not cut through.

- Sprinkle remaining salt on cucumbers. Set aside.

- Combine stuffing ingredients and mix well.

- Gently squeeze excess water from cucumbers or dry with a clean towel. Fill cavity with stuffing.

- Refrigerate stuffed cucumbers for 5–6 hours before serving. The stuffed cucumbers will keep for up to 5 days in the refrigerator.

Press the stuffing into the criss-cross cut of the cucumbers.

DICED RADISH KIMCHI (KKAK-DU-GI)

A kimchi made with radish and seasoned with chilli powder and fish sauce.

INGREDIENTS

White radish	1, large, peeled and cut into 2 x 1.5 cm (1 x 3/4 in) dice
Salt	50 g (1 2/3 oz)
Artificial sweetener	1 tsp
Spring onions (scallions)	2, cut into 2-cm (1-in) lengths
Ginger	2 slices, chopped
Garlic	3 cloves, peeled and crushed
Chilli powder	120 g (4 1/2 oz)
Fish sauce	2 Tbsp

METHOD

- Rinse radish dices and drain well. Toss with salt and sweetener, then leave for 30 minutes. Drain off any excess water from radish. Do not rinse.

- Mix together spring onions, ginger, garlic, chilli powder and fish sauce. Add a pinch of salt if preferred.

- Combine with radish and store in an airtight container for a day before serving.

Cut the radish into 1/2-in (1-cm) thick rounds, then make cuts across 1-cm (1/2-in) apart to get dices.

Place the radish in a large bowl and sprinkle the salt and sweetener over. Toss lightly.

Use gloves when mixing the ingredients. Ensure they are well combined. Store the radish in a clean, airtight container.

PAN-FRIED STUFFED CHILLIES
(GO-CHU-JEON)

Stuffed chillies dipped in beaten egg and lightly fried until golden.

Remove the seeds from the chillies. Wear gloves if your hands are sensitive as chillies tend to leave a burning sensation on skin.

Gently pat the chillies dry using absorbent paper, paying special attention to the cavity of the chillies.

Rub flour into the cavity of the chillies, then use your fingers to press the beef or pork mixture in.

INGREDIENTS

Green chillies	10
Red chillies	1–2 (optional)
Salt	$^3/_4$ Tbsp
Minced beef	50 g ($1^2/_3$ oz)
Minced pork	50 g ($1^2/_3$ oz)
Plain (all-purpose) flour	65 g ($2^1/_2$ oz)
Egg	1
Cooking oil	

SEASONING

Light soy sauce	$^1/_2$ Tbsp
Sugar	$^1/_2$ Tbsp
Chopped spring onion (scallion)	$1^1/_2$ Tbsp
Crushed garlic	1 Tbsp
Sesame oil	1 Tbsp
Ground white pepper	to taste

DIPPING SAUCE

Light soy sauce	1 Tbsp
Water	1 Tbsp
Vinegar	$^1/_2$ Tbsp
Sugar	$^1/_2$ Tbsp

METHOD

- Cut tops off chillies then slice lengthwise in half. Remove seeds and sprinkle with salt. Set aside for 30 minutes, then pat-dry with absorbent paper.

- Combine seasoning ingredients. Divide into 2 portions and separately mix into minced beef and pork.

- Mix dipping sauce ingredients together. Set aside.

- Remove excess moisture from chillies and rub flour into the cavity. Fill with seasoned beef or pork.

- Heat a pan with some oil. Dip stuffed chillies in beaten egg and pan-fry. Do not flip chillies over too often. When meat is slightly browned, remove from heat.

- Serve hot with dipping sauce.

FISH & SEAFOOD

Pan-fried Fish Fillet *(Saeng-Seon-Jeon)*

Pan-fried Seafood with Spring Onion *(Pa-Jeon)*

Chilled Jellyfish with Cucumber *(Hae-Pa-Ri-Nang-Chae)*

Spicy Top Shell *(Gol-Baeng-E-Mu-Chim)*

Grilled Salmon *(Yeon-Eo-Gu-E)*

Stir-fried Octopus *(Nack-Ji-Bock-Kkeum)*

Fried Sea Bream *(Jan-Chi-Do-Mi)*

PAN-FRIED FISH FILLET
(SAENG-SEON-JEON)

Fillet of fish lightly fried until golden brown and crisp.

INGREDIENTS

Fish fillet	1, halved lengthwise, then sliced at an angle
Salt	1 tsp
Ground white pepper	1 tsp
Ginger juice	1/2 Tbsp
Plain (all-purpose) flour	130 g (4 1/2 oz)
Eggs	2, beaten
Cooking oil	125 ml (4 fl oz / 1/2 cup)

VINEGAR SOY SAUCE

Light soy sauce	4 Tbsp
Vinegar	2 Tbsp
Chilli powder	2 tsp
Sesame oil	2 tsp

METHOD

- Season fish with salt, pepper and ginger juice. Leave for 1 hour.

- Meanwhile, combine ingredients for vinegar soy sauce and mix well. Set aside.

- Pat fish dry with absorbent paper, then coat with flour. Dip in beaten egg.

- Heat oil and pan-fry fish over medium heat until golden brown. Garnish as desired and serve hot with vinegar soy sauce.

Hold the knife firmly at an angle and slice fish fillet into small pieces.

Rub seasoning well into fish using your hands.

Dip fish in beaten egg, then gently place into the hot pan to cook.

PAN-FRIED SEAFOOD WITH SPRING ONION (PA-JEON)

A seafood pancake lightly fragranced with spring onion.

Ensure that seafood is well drained of excess juices or the resulting pancakes will be mushy.

Place the coated spring onion lengths close together in an oiled pan.

Pour some batter over spring onion lengths to bind them together into a pancake.

INGREDIENTS

Oysters	10, shucked
Prawns (shrimps)	5, medium, peeled
Clams	10, shelled
Salt	a pinch
Ground white pepper	a pinch
Ginger juice	$^1/_2$ tsp
Spring onions (scallions)	100 g ($3^1/_2$ oz), cut into equal lengths, white portions lightly bruised
Plain (all-purpose) flour for sprinkling	
Vegetable oil	4 Tbsp
Vinegar soy sauce (page 52)	1 recipe

BATTER

Plain (all purpose) flour	130 g ($4^1/_2$ oz / 1 cup)
Rice flour	65 g ($2^1/_2$ oz / $^1/_2$ cup)
Water	375 ml (12 fl oz / $1^1/_2$ cups)
Egg	1

METHOD

- Wash oysters, prawns and clams in brine (mix 625 ml (20 fl oz / 5 cups) water with 1 tsp salt) and drain well.

- Season oysters, prawns and clams with a pinch of salt and pepper and ginger juice. Leave refrigerated for 30 minutes. Drain well, then chop into smaller pieces.

- Combine ingredients for batter with a whisk into a light batter.

- Sprinkle spring onion lengths with some flour. Lower them into batter to coat lightly.

- Transfer spring onion lengths to an oiled pan to cook. Pour some more batter over. Top with seafood. When batter is almost set, pour remaining batter over.

- Flip pancake over and cook other side. Continue to flip and cook until both sides are golden brown in colour.

- Slice and serve wtih vinegar soy sauce.

CHILLED JELLYFISH WITH CUCUMBER
(HAE-PA-RI-NANG-CHAE)

This is a cold appetiser of jellyfish and cucumber mixed in a mustard sauce.

INGREDIENTS

Jellyfish	300 g (11 oz)
Vinegar	3 Tbsp
Salt	2 tsp
Sugar	2 Tbsp
Mustard	2 Tbsp
Crushed garlic	1/2 Tbsp
Lemon	2 slices
Large prawns (shrimps)	4
Cucumber skin	from 1 cucmber, julienned
White sesame seeds	1/2 tsp, roasted

METHOD

- Rinse jellyfish in several changes of cold water to remove any sea salt.

- Place jellyfish in a sieve and pour hot water (about 90°C / 194°F) over. Leave to cool, then squeeze excess water out with your hands.

- Combine vinegar, salt, sugar, mustard and garlic in a mixing bowl. Add jellyfish and refrigerate for 2 hours.

- In a small pot, bring some water to the boil and add lemon and prawns. When prawns turn colour and are cooked, remove and rinse in cold water.

- Peel, then slice each prawn lengthwise into two. Set aside.

- In a mixing bowl, toss jellyfish and cucumber together, then transfer to a plate. Serve cold with prawns and garnish with cucumber shreds.

Carefully skin cucumber with a knife, then julienne. Reserve skinned cucumber for use in other recipes.

Pour hot water over the jellyfish to scald it briefly.

The prawns are cooked when they turn a bright orange colour.

SPICY TOP SHELL (GOL-BAENG-E-MU-CHIM)

Top shells tossed with chopped vegetables in a spicy sauce.

Slice top shell with a sharp knife using firm, even strokes.

Carefully slice away the seeds from the cucumber so the final dish will not be soggy or mushy.

After blending the ingredients for the sauce into a smooth paste, add in sesame seeds and stir to mix well.

INGREDIENTS

Top shell	100 g (3½ oz), sliced
Carrot	½, cut into 3 x 1.5-cm (1½ x ¾-in) pieces
Japanese cucumber	1, seeds removed and cut into 3 x 1.5-cm (1½ x ¾-in) pieces
Round cabbage	4 leaves, cut into 3 x 1.5-m (1½ x ¾-in) pieces
Onion	1, peeled and thinly sliced
Leek	1, cut into thin 4-cm (2-in) lengths
Red chilli	1, cut into thin 4-cm (2-in) lengths
Green chilli	1, cut into thin 4-cm (2-in) lengths

VINEGAR HOT CHILLI PASTE

Hot chilli paste	300 g (11 oz)
Vinegar	125 ml (4 fl oz / ½ cup)
Mineral water	2 Tbsp
Sugar	3 Tbsp
Crushed garlic	3 Tbsp
Mirin	2 Tbsp
Glucose	2 Tbsp
White sesame seeds	2 Tbsp, roasted
Sesame oil	2 Tbsp

METHOD

- Start preparations for vinegar hot chilli paste up to 3 days ahead. Combine all ingredients except sesame oil. Leave to ferment at room temperature for 3 days. Drizzle with sesame oil just before using.

- Mix top shell, carrot, cucumber, cabbage, onion, leek and chillies with vinegar hot chilli paste just before serving. Serve chilled.

GRILLED SALMON (YEON-EO-GU-E)

Seasoned grilled salmon with onion sauce.

INGREDIENTS

Salmon	400 g (14 oz), cut into 2-cm (1-in) thick slices
Coarse salt	1 Tbsp
Ground white pepper	to taste
Cooking oil	3 Tbsp

SAUCE

Light soy sauce	125 ml (4 fl oz / $1/2$ cup)
Sugar	2 Tbsp
Cooking wine	2 Tbsp
Onion	$1/2$, peeled and chopped
Ginger	2–3 slices, chopped

METHOD

- Start preparations up to 8 hours ahead.

- Sprinkle salmon with coarse salt and pepper. Leave for 2 hours.

- Combine ingredients for sauce and mix well with a blender. Strain sauce through a sieve. Discard residue.

- Dry salmon using absorbent paper and place in sauce. Refrigerate for 6 hours.

- Drain salmon. Heat oil and grill. Serve hot with lemon slices and wasabi if desired.

Strain the sauce through a sieve into a container.

Place salmon into the sauce then cover and refrigerate.

Place marinated salmon on a hot grill to cook.

STIR-FRIED OCTOPUS
(NACK-JI-BOCK-KKEUM)

Octopus stir-fried in a hot chilli sauce.

Pour flour onto octopus, then use hands to rub octopus to clean it.

Cut octopus into 5-cm (2-in) pieces.

Stir-fry octopus briefly over high heat. Do not overcook or octopus will be tough.

INGREDIENTS

Octopus	1, about 400 g (14 oz), well-rinsed
Plain (all-purpose) flour	170 g (6 oz / 1 cup)
Hot chilli paste	2 Tbsp
Chilli powder	3 Tbsp
Garlic	1 Tbsp crushed and 1 Tbsp chopped
Light soy sauce	1 Tbsp
Sugar	1 1/2 Tbsp
Ginger juice	1 tsp
Ground white pepper	1 Tbsp
Cooking oil	3 Tbsp
Onion	60 g (2 oz), peeled and cut into 5-cm (2-in) thick slices
Carrot	40 g (1 1/2 oz)
Courgette (zucchini)	60 g (2 oz)
Red chilli	1/2, sliced
Green chilli	1/2, sliced
Sesame oil	1 Tbsp
Leek	a few slices
White sesame seeds	1 tsp, roasted

METHOD

- Coat octopus with flour, then rub to clean it. Rinse well, then cut into 5-cm (2-in) lengths.

- Combine hot chilli paste, chilli powder, crushed garlic, light soy sauce, sugar, ginger juice and pepper. Add octopus and mix well. Set aside.

- Heat oil and stir-fry chopped garlic and onion until fragrant.

- Add carrot, courgette and octopus and quickly stir-fry over high heat.

- Stir in red and green chilli slices and sesame oil, then remove from heat.

- Garnish with leek and sesame seeds before serving with noodles or rice.

FRIED SEA BREAM (JAN-CHI-DO-MI)

Deep-fried sea bream seasoned with sweet soy sauce.

Using a sharp knife, make 3 diagonal cuts on each side of fish to allow marinade to penetrate fish.

Lightly coat fish with corn flour using a small sieve. This will ensure a light, even coating.

Gently lower fried fish into pan without breaking fish.

INGREDIENTS

Sea bream (or red snapper)	1, about 700 g (1 1/2 lb), cleaned
Salt	1 Tbsp
Ground white pepper	2 tsp
Ginger juice	2 tsp
Corn flour (cornstarch)	60 g (2 oz / 1/2 cup)
Cooking oil	250 ml (8 fl oz / 1 cup)
Green capsicum (bell pepper)	1, cored and julienned
Leek	1, cut into 2.5-cm (1-in) lengths
Onion	1, peeled and julienned
Carrot	1, peeled and julienned

SAUCE

Cooking wine	2 Tbsp
Crushed garlic	1/2 Tbsp
Ground white pepper	1 tsp
Light soy sauce	5 Tbsp
Sugar	2 Tbsp
Maltose	2 Tbsp
Water	125 ml (4 fl oz / 1/2 cup)
Mirin	125 ml (4 fl oz / 1/2 cup)

METHOD

- Make 3 shallow cuts on each side of fish. Do not cut through. Sprinkle salt, pepper and ginger juice on fish and leave for 2 hours.

- Combine ingredients for sauce and mix well with a blender. Set aside.

- Drain fish and pat dry using absorbent paper. Sprinkle corn flour over.

- Heat cooking oil in a pan and cook fish on one side. When done, turn fish over to cook the other side.

- In another pan, heat 3 Tbsp cooking oil and add sauce. When sauce comes to the boil, lower fish in. Reduce heat to simmer.

- Top fish with capsicum, leek, onion and carrot and ladle sauce over. fish repeatedly as sauce simmers. Allow sauce to reduce slightly before serving hot.

MEAT & POULTRY

Korean Beef Stir-fry *(Bul-Go-Gi)*

Grilled and Marinated Beef Ribs *(Gal-Bi-Gu-E)*

Braised Short Ribs *(Gal-Bi-Jjim)*

Stir-fried Pork *(Dwae-Ji-Go-Gi-Bok-Keum)*

Pressed Pork *(Dwae-Ji-Go-Gi-Pyeon-Yuk)*

Beef Braised in Soy Sauce *(Jang-Jo-Rim)*

Seasoned and Simmered Chicken *(Dak-Jjim)*

KOREAN BEEF STIR-FRY (BUL-GO-GI)

Tender and juicy beef marinated in light soy sauce.

Teriyaki beef is sliced very thinly by machine.

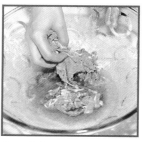

Knead the marinade well into the beef using your hands.

Stir-fry the beef lightly with a pair of chopsticks. Do not overcook the beef.

INGREDIENTS

Cooking oil	$^1/_2$ Tbsp
Minced garlic	3 Tbsp
Carrot	1, sliced
Spring onion (scallion)	1, sliced
Shiitake mushrooms	2, sliced
White sesame seeds	$^1/_2$ tsp, dry-roasted
Sesame oil	a few drops

BEEF STIR-FRY

Teriyaki beef	500 g (1 lb 1$^1/_2$ oz)
Light soy sauce	3 Tbsp
Sugar	90 g (3 oz)
Ground black pepper	1 Tbsp
Canned pineapple rings	2
Canned pear juice or pineapple syrup	125 ml (4 fl oz / $^1/_2$ cup)
Sesame oil	3 Tbsp
Onion	1$^1/_2$, peeled and minced
Mirin	125 ml (4 fl oz / $^1/_2$ cup)

METHOD

- Start preparations a day or at least 2 hours ahead.

- Combine beef stir-fry ingredients in a large mixing bowl. Mix well with your hands. Refrigerate overnight or for at least 2 hours.

- Heat cooking oil and add garlic. When garlic is fragrant, add marinated beef, then sliced carrot, spring onion and mushrooms. Stir-fry lightly.

- Sprinkle in sesame seeds and sesame oil just before removing from heat. Serve hot.

GRILLED AND MARINATED BEEF RIBS (GAL-BI-GU-E)

Marinated beef ribs barbecued to perfection.

INGREDIENTS

Beef ribs	1 kg (2 lb 3 oz), about 10 ribs
Pineapple syrup or	
pear juice (see Note)	125 ml (4 fl oz / $^1/_2$ cup)

MARINADE

Light soy sauce	105 ml ($3^1/_3$ fl oz / 7 Tbsp)
Sugar	3 Tbsp
Ground black pepper	2 Tbsp
Onion	150 g ($5^1/_3$ oz), peeled and chopped
Spring onions (scallions)	3
Crushed garlic	3 Tbsp
Sesame oil	1 Tbsp
Coarsely ground pine nuts	

METHOD

- Start preparations up to a day ahead.

- Soak ribs for 10 minutes, then wash and drain. Tenderise ribs with a meat hammer. This will allow the marinade to penetrate the meat.

- Combine marinade ingredients and blend well. Pour pineapple syrup or pear juice into marinade and mix well.

- Add ribs to marinade and leave to steep for 12 hours.

- Grill ribs until cooked. Garnish with pine nuts and serve.

Note: Pineapple syrup is obtained from canned pineapples. Pear juice is available from Korean supermarkets. You can also grate a pear and squeeze the pulp for juice.

In Korea, the beef ribs used for this recipe are thinly sliced across the rib bones. You can specially order this cut from some butchers or Korean supermarkets.

Drain the syrup from canned pineapples. Reserve the pineapples for use in other recipes.

Cook the ribs over a hot grill. The ribs are cooked when they turn colour.

BRAISED SHORT RIBS (GAL-BI-JJIM)

Ribs simmered in soy sauce over low heat until tender and tasty.

Score the meaty parts of the short ribs to allow the marinade to penetrate the meat.

Angle the knife slightly to slice the mushrooms so they show both the lighter cream colour and the darker brown colour when added to the dish.

When the ribs are tender, add the vegetables to the pot.

Note: Pineapple syrup is obtained from canned pineapples. Pear juice is available from Korean supermarkets. You can also grate a pear and squeeze the pulp for juice.

INGREDIENTS

Beef short ribs	1 kg (2 lb), meaty parts scored
Water	2 litres (64 fl oz / 8 cups)
Dried shiitake mushrooms	8, soaked for 10 minutes, squeezed dry and sliced, steams discarded
Carrots	2, medium, cut into small pieces
Chestnuts	6, shelled
Dried red dates	1–2 stoned and sliced

MARINADE

Light soy sauce	105 ml (3^1/$_2$ oz / 7 Tbsp)
Sugar	3 Tbsp
Crushed garlic	2 Tbsp
Sesame oil	1 Tbsp
Pineapple syrup or pear juice	150 ml (5 fl oz / 10 Tbsp)
Cooking wine	2 Tbsp
Ground black pepper	1 Tbsp
Spring onions (scallions)	2, chopped

METHOD

- Soak ribs for 20 minutes, changing the water several times. Drain and trim fat from ribs.

- Combine marinade ingredients and place ribs in to marinate for 1 hour.

- Place marinated ribs in a heavy-based pot. Add water and cook over medium heat until ribs are tender. Takes 30–40 minutes.

- Add mushrooms, carrots and chestnuts, then reduce heat to simmer for 20–30 minutes. Serve hot, garnished with red dates.

STIR-FRIED PORK
(DWAE-JI-GO-GI-BOK-KEUM)

Pork marinated with red chilli pepper paste and stir-fried.

INGREDIENTS

Pork shoulder	1 kg (2 lb 3 oz), machine-sliced into teriyaki-thin strips
Hot chilli paste	4 Tbsp
Light soy sauce	2 Tbsp
Sugar	2 Tbsp
Ground black pepper	$1/2$ Tbsp
Crushed garlic	2 Tbsp
Ginger juice	1 tsp
Chilli powder	2 Tbsp
Pineapple syrup	125 ml (4 fl oz / $1/2$ cup)
Onion	1, medium, peeled and sliced
White sesame seeds	1 tsp, roasted

METHOD

- Start preparations up to 6 hours ahead.

- Combine all ingredients except onion, sesame seeds and sliced chilli. Leave pork to marinate for 6 hours.

- Heat some cooking oil and pan-fry marinated pork until almost cooked. Add onion and continue to cook until well done.

- Sprinkle sesame seeds over and garnish as desired before serving.

Marinate the pork for at least 6 hours. The pork will absorb the flavours and take on a lovely reddish colour from the chilli paste.

When the pork is cooked, add the onion and continue to stir-fry until the onions are soft.

Sprinkle the sesame seeds over the cooked dish with your fingers to distribute them more evenly. Roasted sesame seeds add fragrance to cooked dishes.

PRESSED PORK
(DWAE-JI-GO-GI-PYEON-YUK)

Pork boiled in a fermented soy paste stock.

Lower pork into the stock gently so as not to cause the stock to splash up.

Wrap the pork tightly with plastic wrap.

Slice the pork into thin, even slices with a sharp knife.

INGREDIENTS

Belly pork	500 g (1 lb 1¹/₂ oz)
Water	2.5 litres (80 fl oz / 10 cups)
Fermented soy paste (*doen-jang*)	2 Tbsp
Light soy sauce	2 Tbsp
Sugar	2 Tbsp
Black peppercorns	1 Tbsp
Garlic	4 cloves, peeled and cut in half
Ginger	4 slices
Korean preserved prawns (shrimps) (optional)	
White sesame seeds	¹/₂ tsp, roasted

LEEK SALAD

Leek	1–2 stalks, shredded
Salt	to taste
Chilli powder	to taste

METHOD

- Soak pork in cold water for 30 minutes, then wash and drain.

- Combine water, fermented soy paste, soy sauce, sugar, black peppercorns, garlic and ginger in a heavy-based pot. Add pork and cook for 20–30 minutes.

- Drain and remove pork from pot. Wrap in plastic wrap and place flat on a worktop. Place a heavy object on pork and leave in a cool place for 30 minutes to 1 hour.

- Remove plastic wrap and slice pork thinly.

- Combine leek salad ingredients.

- Serve pork with leek salad and preserved pawns, if desired. Garnish with sesame seeds.

BEEF BRAISED IN SOY SAUCE (JANG-JO-RIM)

A side dish of beef braised in soy sauce and garlic.

INGREDIENTS

Garlic	4–5 cloves
Onion	¹/₂, peeled
Black peppercorns	2 tsp
Water	1.25 litres (40 fl oz / 5 cups)
Beef	500 g (1 lb 1¹/₂ oz)
Light soy sauce	190 ml (6 fl oz / ³/₄ cup)
Sugar	3 Tbsp
Hardboiled eggs	2–3, peeled and sliced
Sesame oil	a few drops

METHOD

- Boil garlic, onion, and peppercorns in water for about 10 minutes.

- Add beef and boil for another 10–20 minutes.

- Test to see if beef is cooked by piercing with a skewer. Drain beef and reserve stock. Discard garlic, onion and peppercorns.

- Place beef and stock in a pot and add soy sauce and sugar. Bring to the boil for 10–15 minutes over medium heat. Remove from heat and leave to cool.

- Slice beef into thin slices and arrange on a bed of hardboiled eggs. Drizzle with sesame oil before serving.

Note: Any leftover sauce can be reserved and used as mild soy sauce.

Test to see if the beef is cooked by piercing it with a skewer. If the juices run clear, the beef is cooked.

Use a sawing motion to cut the cooked beef into thin, even slices.

When hardboiling eggs, place into water at room temperature, then bring to the boil for 8–10 minutes. Allow to cool before cracking and peeling off the shell.

SEASONED AND SIMMERED CHICKEN
(DAK-JJIM)

A sweet and spicy chicken dish with onions, carrots and potatoes.

Combine the ingredients for the seasoning and mix well. You should get a watery paste once the water is added.

When the chicken is half-cooked, pour in half the seasoning mixture and stir to coat the chicken.

Lower the onions, carrots and potatoes gently into the boiling chicken mixture and stir to mix the ingredients.

INGREDIENTS

Cooking oil	$^1/_2$ Tbsp
Whole chicken	1, 800 g–1 kg (1$^3/_4$ lb–2 lb 3 oz), cleaned and cut into 4-cm (2-in) pieces
Big onions	300 g (11 oz), peeled and cut into 3-cm (1$^1/_2$-in) cubes
Carrots	100 g (3$^1/_2$ oz), cut into 3-cm (1$^1/_2$-in) cubes
Potatoes	200 g (7 oz), peeled and cut into 3-cm (1$^1/_2$-in) cubes
Leek	a few slices
Green chilli	a few slices

SEASONING

Light soy sauce	2 Tbsp
Crushed garlic	2 Tbsp
Hot chilli paste	1 Tbsp
Chilli powder	2 Tbsp
Ginger juice	1 Tbsp
Ground black pepper	2 tsp
Sugar	2 Tbsp
Sesame oil	1 tsp (optional)
Water	125 ml (4 fl oz / $^1/_2$ cup)

METHOD

- Combine seasoning ingredients adding water last. Mix well. Set aside.

- Heat oil until hot but not smoking and fry chicken for about 7 minutes.

- Pour in half the seasoning mixture and boil for 10 minutes.

- Add onions, carrots and potatoes and remaining seasoning mixture. Continue boiling until chicken is tender but vegetables are not mushy. Lower heat to simmer for 20 minutes.

- Garnish with leek and green chilli. Serve hot with steamed rice.

RICE & NOODLES

Rice Mixed with Vegetables and Beef *(Bi-Bim-Bap)*

Pumpkin Porridge *(Ho-Bak-Juk)*

Sweet Potato Noodles *(Jab-Chae)*

Cold Noodles *(Guksu-Nang-Guk)*

Noodle Salad *(Salad-Guksu)*

Fried Rice Cake with Spicy Sauce *(Tteok-Bok-Ki)*

Sliced Rice Cake in Soup *(Tteok-Guk)*

RICE MIXED WITH VEGETABLES AND BEEF (BI-BIM-BAP)

Rice topped with beef and vegetables and served with a chilli paste.

Hold the knife at a 45° angle to slice the mushrooms in half before you julienne them. This way, there will be some dark and some light coloured strips for better presentation.

Use your hands to gently squeeze the bean sprouts to remove excess water before seasoning them.

Crack the egg into a hot, oiled pan and allow it to cook through. Do not flip the egg over.

INGREDIENTS

Japanese rice	450 g (1 lb)
Ground or chopped beef	100 g (3 1/2 oz)
Cooking oil	1 tsp
Courgette (zucchini)	1/2, peeled and julienned
Carrots	1/2, peeled and julienned
Shiitake mushrooms	2, julienned, stems discarded
Bean sprouts	30 g (1 oz), parboiled in lightly salted water and squeezed dry
Egg	1, cooked, sunny-side up

BEEF SEASONING

Light soy sauce	2 tsp
Ground black pepper	a pinch
Sugar	1 tsp
Minced garlic	1 tsp
Sesame oil	2 tsp

BEAN SPROUTS SEASONING

Salt	1/2 tsp
Spring onion (scallion)	1
Garlic	2 cloves, peeled and minced
Sesame oil	1 tsp
White sesame seeds	1 tsp, roasted

CHILLI PASTE WITH SESAME (OPTIONAL)

Hot chilli paste	4 Tbsp
White sesame seeds	1 Tbsp, roasted
Sesame oil	2 tsp

PAN-BROILED CHILLI PASTE (OPTIONAL)

Cooking oil	2 Tbsp
Minced beef	700 g (1 1/2 lb)
Light soy sauce	1 Tbsp
Ground white pepper	2 Tbsp
Sugar	180 g (6 1/2 oz)
Hot chilli paste	1 kg (2 lb)
Mirin	375 ml (12 fl oz / 3/4 cup)
Glucose	8–10 Tbsp
Pine nuts	1 Tbsp

METHOD

- Wash rice, then soak for 30 minutes and drain. Cook rice in a rice cooker with 500 ml (16 fl oz / 2 cups) water.

- Combine beef with beef seasoning, then stir-fry lightly until cooked.

- Heat oil in a frying pan and stir-fry courgette quickly so the colour stays vivid. Remove. Stir-fry carrots and mushrooms in the same way.

- Sprinkle bean sprouts seasoning over parboiled bean sprouts.

- Prepare chilli paste with sesame or pan-broiled chilli paste. For chilli paste with sesame, combine ingredients and use as needed. For pan-broiled chilli paste, heat oil and sauté minced beef. Add soy sauce, pepper and sugar. Add hot chilli paste and mirin and cook well. Add glucose and some pine nuts. Taste and ensure that it is sweet and hot. Remove from heat and leave to cool. Refrigerate and use as needed.

- Arrange beef, vegetables and egg in a bowl. Serve accompanied with rice, chilli paste with sesame or pan-broiled chilli paste.

PUMPKIN PORRIDGE (HO-BAK-JUK)

This is a classic Korean pumpkin porridge. Kidney beans or sweet pear are often added for extra texture and flavour.

INGREDIENTS

Glutinous rice	2 Tbsp, soaked for 1 hour, then drained
Pumpkin	400 g (14 oz), peeled, washed and steamed
Water	250 ml (8 fl oz / 1 cup)
Salt	1/2 Tbsp
Sugar	2 Tbsp

METHOD

- Grind glutinous rice in a blender with 125 ml (4 fl oz / 1/2 cup) water. Remove and set aside.

- Purée steamed pumpkin in a blender with remaining water. Remove and set aside.

- Place ground glutinous rice mixture in a heavy pot and bring to the boil, stirring occasionally. Add puréed pumpkin and simmer for 15 minutes.

- Add salt and sugar, then return to the boil before serving.

The ground glutinous rice should be a milky white liquid with some residue.

Cut the pumpkin into smaller pieces, then slice the skin off with a knife.

After steaming, the pumpkin should take on a darker hue and be soft and tender.

SWEET POTATO NOODLES (JAB-CHAE)

This is a dish which is usually prepared for festive occasions. Sweet potato noodles do not keep well, so cook just enough for serving.

After stir-frying the ingredients, it is important to spread them out to cool thoroughly, otherwise they will break into small pieces when stir-fried again.

Cut the noodles into short lengths with a pair of kitchen scissors. This makes it easier to handle when eating.

Stir-fry the beef and mushrooms lightly. The beef is cooked when it changes colour.

INGREDIENTS

Fresh or dried shittake mushrooms	3
Beef	30 g (1 oz), thinly sliced
Onion	30 g (1 oz), peeled and julienned
Carrot	20 g (1 oz), julienned
Green capsicum (bell pepper)	1, small, cored and julienned
Salt	to taste
Dried sweet potato noodles (*dang-myeon*)	50 g (1²/₃ oz)
White sesame seeds	1 tsp, roasted

SAUCE A

Light soy sauce	2 Tbsp
Sugar	1 Tbsp
Minced garlic	2 tsp
Sesame oil	2 tsp
White sesame seeds	2 tsp, roasted

SAUCE B

Light soy sauce	2 Tbsp
Sugar	2 Tbsp
Sesame oil	2 Tbsp

METHOD

- If using dried mushrooms, soak in warm water for 10 minutes to soften, then squeeze dry and julienne. If using fresh mushrooms, julienne.

- Season beef and mushrooms with sauce A.

- Separately stir-fry onion, carrot and capsicum in a lightly oiled pan. Sprinkle with salt to taste each time. Spread on a large plate to cool.

- Using the same pan, stir-fry seasoned beef and mushrooms.

- Boil noodles until soft, then drain and cut into short lengths. Mix in sauce B.

- Stir-fry noodles lightly, then add beef and vegetables and continue to stir-fry until beef is done. Dish out and garnish with sesame seeds.

COLD NOODLES (GUKSU-NANG-GUK)

This cold noodle dish is often served during summer in Korea.

Fry the anchovies in a dry pan until they are completely dry and lightly crisp.

After cooking the noodles, rinse them in ice-cold water to stop the cooking process. The noodles will remain crisp.

Mix the chopped kimchi with sugar, salt and sesame oil. Use a pair of chopsticks to mix thoroughly.

INGREDIENTS

White wheat noodles	400 g (14 oz)
Kimchi	200 g (7 oz), chopped
Sugar	1 Tbsp
Salt	1 Tbsp
Sesame oil	1 tsp, optional
Anchovy stock	750 ml (24 fl oz / 3 cups), chilled
Kimchi brine	125 ml (4 fl oz / $^1/_2$ cup)
Vinegar	1 Tbsp
Mustard	1 Tbsp
Cucumber	1, sliced
Hardboiled eggs	2, peeled and sliced
Lettuce	$^1/_2$ head, finely sliced
Pine nuts	3 Tbsp

SAUTÉED DRIED ANCHOVIES

Dried anchovies	50 g ($1^2/_3$ oz)
Cooking wine	1 Tbsp
Light soy sauce	1 Tbsp
Sugar	1 Tbsp
Cooking oil	1 Tbsp
Sesame oil	1 Tbsp
Maltose	1 Tbsp

METHOD

- Prepare sautéed dried anchovies. Dry-fry anchovies over low heat until dry. Add cooking wine and continue frying until anchovies are dry again. Remove from heat. Combine soy sauce, sugar, cooking oil, sesame oil and maltose and bring to the boil. Turn off the heat and mix in anchovies. Set aside until needed.

- Bring noodles to the boil in some water. Drain then rinse noodles under running water before plunging into ice-cold water. Drain noodles in a sieve.

- Mix kimchi with sugar, salt and sesame oil. Set aside.

- Place noodles in a pot with cold anchovy stock and kimchi brine. Stir in vinegar and mustard. Mix well.

- Dish noodles out into individual bowls and top with cucumber, eggs, lettuce and kimchi. Sprinkle with pine nuts and serve with sautéed dried anchovies in a separate saucer.

NOODLE SALAD (SALAD-GUKSU)

Cold noodles mixed with vegetables in a spicy sauce.

INGREDIENTS

Soba noodles	2 bundles
Cabbage or lettuce	5 leaves, cut into thin 4-cm (2-in) lengths
Cucumber	1, medium, cut into thin 4-cm (2-in) lengths
Carrot	$^1/_2$, cut into thin 4-cm (2-in) lengths
Cherry tomatoes	10, each cut in half
Crabsticks	4, shredded

SAUCE

Light soy sauce	3 Tbsp
Vinegar	3 Tbsp
Lemon juice	3 Tbsp
Sugar	4 Tbsp
Oyster sauce	$^1/_2$ Tbsp
Crushed garlic	1 Tbsp
Wasabi	$1^1/_2$ tsp
Chilli powder	1 Tbsp
Sesame oil	1 Tbsp

METHOD

- Combine ingredients for sauce and blend well. Refrigerate to chill

- Blanch noodles in boiling water, then wash under cold running water. Drain well.

- Mix noodles with chilled sauce and some vegetables and crabsticks.

- Garnish with remaining vegetables and crabsticks and serve.

To cut cabbage or lettuce leaves, roll a few leaves up and slice thinly.

Shred the crabsticks by peeling it strip by strip, layer by layer. It will come apart quite easily.

Mix the noodles with the chilled sauce using your hands to ensure a more thorough mix.

FRIED RICE CAKE WITH SPICY SAUCE (TTEOK-BOK-KI)

Rice cakes cooked in a spicy-sweet sauce with mixed vegetables.

INGREDIENTS

Cooking oil	2 Tbsp
Hot chilli paste	2 Tbsp
Chilli powder	1/2 Tbsp
Beef seasoning powder	1 1/2 tsp (optional)
Sugar	1 1/2 Tbsp
Frozen Korean rice cake rolls	200 g (7 oz), cut in half
Water	180 ml (6 fl oz / 3/4 cup)
Fish cakes (*eo-muk*)	70 g (2 1/2 oz), sliced
Cabbage leaves	3, sliced
White sesame seeds	1 tsp, roasted
Spring onion (scallion) or leek	1, sliced

METHOD

- Heat a wok for 5 minutes, then add cooking oil. Add hot chilli paste, chilli and beef powder, sugar and rice cake rolls. Stir-fry for 5 minutes over medium heat.

- Add water, fish cakes and cabbage and simmer for 10 minutes.

- Dish out and garnish with sesame seeds and spring onion or leek.

Rinse the rice cake rolls with water, then cut into halves. You do not need to thaw the rice cake rolls.

You can use any kind of fish cake for this dish. Cut the fish cakes into slices.

Stir-fry the ingredients to mix them and coat the rice cake rolls and fish cakes with sauce.

SLICED RICE CAKE IN SOUP
(TTEOK-GUK)

Korean rice cake in a light beef stock. This festive dish is eaten to celebrate the new year in Korea.

INGREDIENTS

Beef	300 g (11 oz)
Garlic	2 cloves
Water	2.5 litres (80 fl oz / 10 cups)
Ground black pepper	1 tsp
Light soy sauce	1 Tbsp
Salt	2 tsp
Sesame oil	1 tsp
Frozen rice cake slices	125 g (4¹/₂ oz)
Spring onion (scallion)	1, sliced
Egg	1, separated and fried into thin omelettes, then thinly sliced

METHOD

- Place beef, garlic and water in a pot and bring to the boil. Reduce heat and simmer for 30–40 minutes.

- Drain beef and thinly slice. Season with pepper, soy sauce, 1 tsp salt and sesame oil and set aside.

- Season beef stock to taste with remaining salt, then bring to the boil. When stock starts to boil, add rice cakes and cook for 20 minutes.

- Return beef to the stock and return to the boil. Add spring onion.

- Ladle rice cakes, beef and stock into individual bowls. Top with sliced omelette and serve hot.

Cut the cooked beef into slices, then slice again thinly.

Add the rice cake slices to the boiling stock and allow to cook for about 20 minutes.

Fry the egg yolk and egg white separately into thin omelettes before slicing thinly.

APPETISERS &
DESSERTS

Sweet Glutinous Rice *(Yak-Sik)*

Water Chestnut Flour Jelly *(Muk-Mu-Chim)*

Sweet and Sour White Radish *(Mu-Cho-Mal-E)*

Cinnamon Punch with Dried Persimmon *(Su-Jeong-Gwa)*

Sweet Rice Cake *(In-Jeol-Mi)*

SWEET GLUTINOUS RICE (YAK-SIK)

Glutinous rice steamed with chestnuts, dried red dates, sugar, pine nuts and cinnamon.

INGREDIENTS

Glutinous rice	630 g (1 lb 6 oz / 3 cups)
Molasses	200 g (7 oz / 1 cup)
Water	500 ml (16 fl oz /2 cups)
Light soy sauce	2 Tbsp
Ground cinnamon	1 tsp
Sesame oil	4 Tbsp
Dried red dates	10, stoned and sliced
Chestnuts	10, peeled and sliced
Pine nuts	1 Tbsp

METHOD

- Soak glutinous rice in water for at least 3 hours.

- Melt molasses in an uncovered pressure cooker over low heat with water, soy sauce, ground cinnamon and sesame oil.

- Drain glutinous rice. Add to pressure cooker with dried red dates, chestnuts and pine nuts.

- Cover pressure cooker and increase heat.

- When pressure cooker starts to steam, switch it off and leave covered for another 3–5 minutes. When all the steam has escaped from the pressure cooker, open the lid and remove glutinous rice.

- Portion rice into small moulds and turn out onto a serving plate. Serve hot or at room temperature.

Combine the molasses with water, soy sauce, ground cinnamon and sesame oil in a pressure cooker over low heat until the molasses is melted.

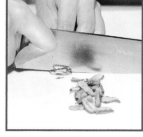

Slice the red dates in half lengthwise, then cut into thin slices.

Compact the rice tightly into the moulds so they will hold their shape when removed from the mould.

WATER CHESTNUT FLOUR JELLY (MUK-MU-CHIM)

A firm jelly appetiser made of water chestnut flour.

Bring the chestnut flour, water and oil mixture to the boil, stirring. Use a whisk to help dissolve the flour.

When set, the jelly will be firm and can be lifted out of the mould easily.

INGREDIENTS

PANCAKE BATTER

Water chestnut flour	60 g (2 oz)
Water	875 ml (28 fl oz / 3¹/₂ cups)
Cooking oil	1 Tbsp
Red chilli	1, sliced
Green chilli	1, sliced
Cucumber	1, small, cut into 4-cm (2-in) lengths
Onion	¹/₂, peeled, cut into 4-cm (2-in) lengths
Chrysanthemum leaves	3, cut into 4-cm (2-in) lengths
Spring onions (scallions)	3, cut into 4-cm (2-in) lengths

SAUCE

Light soy sauce	2 Tbsp
Fish sauce	2 Tbsp
Sugar	¹/₂ Tbsp
Chilli powder	¹/₂ Tbsp
Vinegar	¹/₂ Tbsp
Crushed garlic	¹/₂ Tbsp
Sesame oil	1 tsp
White sesame seeds	1 Tbsp, roasted
Sesame oil	a few drops

METHOD

- Dissolve chestnut flour in water. Add cooking oil and bring to the boil, stirring. Lower heat and continue stirring until mixture is thick.

- Pour mixture into an oiled rectangular mould and leave to set.

- Combine sauce ingredients and refrigerate.

- When chestnut jelly is set, remove from mould and cut into rectangular slices.

- Mix jelly with chilled sauce, chillies, cucumber, onion, chrysanthemum leaves and spring onions. Serve chilled.

SWEET AND SOUR WHITE RADISH
(MU-CHO-MAL-E)

A refreshing appetiser of marinated radish.

Dip the radish slices into the salt and sugar solution and leave for 6 hours.

Pat-dry the radish slices gently with absorbent paper.

Place strips of cucumber skin, pear and carrot on a slice of radish and roll up. Sit rolls on the exposed edge so they do not come undone.

INGREDIENTS

Water	250 ml (8 fl oz / 1 cup)
Salt	1 Tbsp
Sugar	1 Tbsp
White radish	$^1/_2$, peeled and thinly sliced into rounds
Cucumber skin	from 1 cucumber, juilenned
Pear	1, juilenned
Carrot	$^1/_2$, peeled and juilenned

MARINADE

Vinegar	2 Tbsp
Water	500 ml (16 fl oz / 2 cups)
Sugar	2 Tbsp
Salt	1 tsp

METHOD

- Start preparations up to a day ahead.

- Combine water, salt and sugar in a bowl. Put radish slices into bowl and leave for 6 hours.

- Drain radish and pat dry using absorbent paper.

- Place a few strips of cucumber skin, pear and carrot on each slice of radish and roll up.

- Combine marinade ingredients and sprinkle over radish rolls. Refrigerate for at least 12 hours before serving.

CINNAMON PUNCH WITH DRIED PERSIMMON (SU-JEONG-GWA)

Cinnamon and ginger punch with dried persimmons makes a refreshing dessert.

INGREDIENTS

Ginger	50 g (1²/₃ oz), peeled and thinly sliced
Water	2 litres (64 fl oz / 8 cups)
Cinnamon sticks	30 g (1 oz)
Brown sugar	175 g (6 oz / 1 cup)
Dried seedless persimmons	3, medium, calyx discarded
Pine nuts	2 tsp

METHOD

- Put ginger and water in a large saucepan. Bring to the boil, then lower heat and simmer for 20–30 minutes.

- Add cinnamon sticks and return to the boil.

- Strain water through a fine sieve. Discard ginger and cinnamon sticks. Stir in sugar.

- Bring water to the boil to dissolve sugar. When sugar has melted, leave liquid to cool.

- Place persimmons into ginger and cinnamon liquid. Leave for 2 hours.

- Cut persimmons into smaller pieces then place into cooled cinnamon and ginger liquid. Serve garnished with pine nuts.

To peel ginger skin, hold the ginger down on a chopping board and lightly scrape away the thin skin using a small paring knife.

Place the dried persimmons into the cooled liquid to soak for 2 hours.

Remove the soaked persimmons and cut into smaller pieces to serve.

SWEET RICE CAKE (IN-JEOL-MI)

Steamed glutinous rice cake coated in soy bean powder.

INGREDIENTS

Glutinous rice flour	500 g (1 lb 1½ oz), sifted
Sugar	90 g (3 oz)
Salt	1½ Tbsp
Water	625 ml (20 fl oz / 2½ cups)
Soy bean powder	10 Tbsp
Honey (optional)	

METHOD

- Mix glutinous rice flour with sugar, salt and water to form a paste.

- Line a steamer with a clean muslin cloth. Pour flour paste onto cloth and steam for 45 minutes.

- Spread soy bean powder on a large plate. Remove steamed cake from muslin cloth and place onto powder to coat.

- Slice coated cake and serve hot or cold with honey (optional).

Mix the flour, sugar, salt and water into a paste. Ensure that the flour is well mixed and that there are no lumps in the paste.

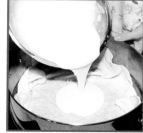

Pour the paste into a steaming tray lined with a muslin cloth.

Scrape the cake off from the muslin cloth using a spatula and coat the cake well with soy bean powder.

GLOSSARY & INDEX

GLOSSARY

CHRYSANTHEMUM LEAVES

These edible leaves are different from those of the chrysanthemum flower grown for display. The leaves are tender and require only light cooking. If unavailable, use your preferred leafy green vegetable.

DRIED ANCHOVIES, SMALL

These small dried anchovies are commonly available in markets and supermarkets. They are not as strong in flavour as the large dried anchovies, but due to their easy availability, they are often used in recipes that call for dried anchovies.

COARSE SALT

Salt is mined from large salt lakes or the sea. A variety of different kinds of salts exists for various purposes. Coarse salt or rock salt, as it is also known, is slightly greyish in colour when compared with other salts. This is because it is not as refined as other salts and contains more minerals and impurities. In Korean cooking, it is used for pickling vegetables.

DRIED ANCHOVIES, LARGE

These dried anchovies are significantly larger than the common dried anchovies available in Chinatowns the world over. The smallest can be at least 5-cm (2-in) long. They are used to flavour soups and stocks and discarded thereafter. You can use the more common, but smaller dried anchovies if these are not available, although the flavour will not be as robust or satisfying.

DRIED PRAWNS (SHRIMPS)

These are the Korean variety of dried prawns. They are of a higher grade than the Chinese dried prawns and cannot be satisfactorily substituted with the latter. Many grades of dried prawns are available in the market or supermarket. Always choose the premium grade of dried prawns whenever possible, as lesser grades tend to be saltier or have a fishy flavour. Since dried prawns vary in quality and flavour, taste the dish and adjust the amount of dried prawns added to your personal preference.

DRIED SEAWEED

Seaweed is a sea plant that belongs to the algae family. This deep green seaweed is a rich source of iodine and is also rich in other minerals and vitamins. Seaweed is commonly used in Japanese and Korean cooking and a variety of different types exists. Dried seaweed has a slight crunchy texture when reconstituted.

DRIED SWEET POTATO NOODLES

As its name suggests, these noodles are made from the sweet potato. They are commonly used in Korean cooking and are available from Korean supermarkets. Long and thin, these noodles resemble angel hair pasta but for its colour. When boiled or cooked, these noodles become translucent. If unavailable, use glass vermicelli.

GINSENG

Also known as Korean ginseng, this is one of the most popular medicinal herbs in the world. It has been used for thousands of years to promote good health and is popularly used to lower cholesterol, increase energy levels and stimulate the immune system. Ginseng is easily available from Chinese medical stores as well as some health food stores.

DRIED SEEDLESS PERSIMMONS

These are persimmons that have either been dried in the sun or wind (air-dried). They have a sweet and chewy texture and can be enjoyed as a tasty snack on their own or cooked in desserts. Dried persimmons have a light coating of flour that prevents them from sticking to each other. This coating is tasteless and can be easily washed off with water.

GLUTINOUS RICE

You can differentiate glutinous rice grains from regular long grain rice by their opaque off-white colour. The rice does not contain gluten as its name suggests, but when cooked, it becomes sticky and is used in both sweet and savoury dishes. Glutinous rice is commonly used in Asian cooking in both sweet and savoury dishes.

HOT CHILLI PASTE

This is a special type of chilli paste from Korea. It cannot be replaced with other types of chilli paste otherwise the taste of the dish will be different. It is commonly used in Korean cooking and is easily available from Korean supermarkets.

MALTOSE

Also known as malt sugar, this thick golden-coloured syrup is available bottled from Asian supermarkets. It has a thick consistency like honey, but it is not as sweet. It is used to add sweetness to dishes.

PINE NUTS

Pine nuts are harvested from pine cones and are popularly used in salads and pasta dishes. These plump tear-shaped seeds are rich in fats and should be stored in the refrigerator or freezer to prevent them from spoiling easily.

RICE CAKES, SLICES AND ROLLS

Made of rice flour, water and salt, these rice cakes are available from the frozen section of Korean supermarkets. They have a firm chewy texture and take on the flavour of the dish readily. The Chinese also have a variety of rice cakes similar to these, but the taste and texture are slightly different.

PRESERVED PRAWNS (SHRIMPS)

These preserved prawns are different from the preserved prawns used in other types of Asian cooking. They are larger in size and very much sweeter than the common Asian variety. As such, they cannot be used as substitutes for each other. Preserved prawns are commonly used in Korean cooking and are thus readily available from Korean supermarkets.

RED CHILLI POWDER

Like the hot chilli paste, this deep red powder is a very special type of chilli powder from Korea. It is of a higher grade than other types of chilli powder and should preferably not be replaced if possible. If unavailable, however, you can use other types of chilli powder, but the amounts to be added to the recipe will vary. Taste and adjust to taste when using other types of chilli powder.

PUMPKINS

Pumpkins have a hard outer skin and can vary in colour and size. The small variety is used here. The skin is green with patches of yellow, and the flesh is a deep, rich yellow. Peel off the skin by slicing with a knife then scrape off the pith and seeds from the centre of the pumpkin before use. When cooked, pumpkin becomes soft and is sweet.

SESAME OIL

Extracted from roasted white sesame seeds, two varieties of this oil exist. One is lighter in colour and the other is darker in colour. In this book, the darker variety is used. It has a rich brownish colour and a strong fragrance. It is generally used to enhance the flavour of dishes in Asian cooking. High in polyunsaturated fats, sesame oil is a healthy cooking oil.

SOY BEAN PASTE

Made from fermented soy beans, this is another special paste from the Korean kitchen. Although the Asian soy bean paste goes by the same name, it is different in flavour and should not be substituted in Korean recipes. This soy bean paste is mild in flavour and sweet. It is a common ingredient used in Korean cooking and is available at Korean supermarkets.

SOY BEAN POWDER

Also known as soy flour, soy bean powder is made from finely ground soy beans. This dark cream coloured flour is high in protein and is commonly used in desserts and other confections in Japan and Korea. It is relatively tasteless on its own and can be mixed with sugar for sweetness.

WATER CHESTNUT FLOUR

Obtained from ground dried water chestnuts, this flour is used as a thickening agent, much like corn flour (cornstarch). It is available in Asian supermarkets and health food stores. If unavailable, substitute with potato flour or corn flour.

WHITE RADISH

This is the root of a plant belonging to the mustard family. White radishes are elongated and are usually larger in diameter than the common orange carrot. Radishes are available all year round. Choose radishes that are firm to the touch. Peel off the skin and trim off the caps and root ends as you would carrots before using.

WHITE WHEAT NOODLES

This is a pale coloured noodle made of wheat flour. They are sold as long thin strands and in bundles. They are easily reconstituted when boiled in water, but do not overcook. If unavailable, substitute with other Asian wheat noodles.

WHITE SESAME SEEDS, ROASTED

These tear-drop shaped seeds are mainly used to garnish and flavour dishes. They have a distinct flavour which is enhanced when roasted. In Korean cooking, white sesame seeds are roasted without oil and left to brown slightly. They are then added as a garnish after the dish is cooked. Vary the amount added to your personal preference.

INDEX